Table of Contents

I0438226

Surviving as a common thread.

A look at what connections exist among therapeutic approaches.

A useful explanation of transference to help in understanding classical approaches to therapy. It is a Freudian concept.

Biological Basis of Mood Disorders

The various mood episodes have different criteria. In Major Depressive Episodes, five or more symptoms must be present for most of the day on more days than not over the course of two or more weeks. Those symptoms include: depressed mood, anhedonia (a lack of pleasure), weight loss or appetite disturbance, sleep disturbance, psychomotor agitation or retardation, fatigue or a loss of energy, feelings of worthlessness or guilt, problems with concentration or decision-making, and thoughts of death or suicidal ideation. This symptoms do not have to be present everyday but must be present for more days than not and for most of the time during those days. Additionally, it is required that at least one of the symptoms must be either a depressed mood or a loss of interest or pleasure. Bereavement, drug abuse, or a general medical condition cannot better account for the symptoms unless the symptoms are greater than that which would be expected by these conditions. The client also may not meet the criteria for a Mixed Episode during this time period.

A Manic Episode is a distinct period of abnormally and persistently elevated, expansive, or irritable mood that also has at least three or more symptoms that last for at least one week or less if hospitalization is needed. The three or more symptoms that are needed for a manic episode include inflated self-esteem or grandiosity, decreased need for sleep, pressured speech, racing thoughts, distractibility, increase in goal-directed activities, excessive involvement in pleasurable activities that are potentially risky. Like the Major Depressive Episode, a Manic Episode must not meet the criteria for a Mixed Episode. The disturbance involves a significant impairment in social or occupational functioning. Individuals suffering from a Manic Episode often need to be hospitalized to prevent harm to self or others.

A Hypomanic Episode has the same criteria that a Manic Episode has but the episode is shorter than a week but at least four days. The individual suffering from a Hypomanic Episode's symptoms are not severe enough to warrant hospitalization. The Hypomanic Episode is also not severe enough to result in impairment in social or occupational functioning and there are no psychotic features associated with the Hypomanic Episodes.

Mixed Episodes are very rare. These episodes meet the criteria for both a Major Depressive Episode and a Manic Episode nearly every day for a week. This means that the required criteria of a Major Depressive Episode and a Manic Episode are occurring during the same day. This does not mean that one day is manic and the next is depressive for a week, but that nearly every day has both the symptoms of a Major Depressive Episode and a Manic Episode for a week.

Depression and Bipolar Disorder have several biological predispositions that result in the symptomology of the two conditions. With the mood disorders, the hypothalamic-adrenal system (HPA-axis) serves as the part of the nervous system that functions in an abnormal manner to produce the symptoms of the two conditions. The HPA-axis serves as the body's reactionary system to stress. The hypothalamus sends signals to the pituitary gland to release hormones into the blood stream to start the process. The pituitary gland releases adrenocorticotropin (ACTH) into the body. ACTH activates a process in the adrenal glands that produces another hormone called cortisol. Cortisol produces the sensations in the body that an individual associates with stress. As the cortisol flows through the body, the brain shuts off the flow of ACTH to stop the release of cortisol. In the case of depressed individual, the feedback system fails, and cortisol continues to be released into the body creating chronic stress and the symptoms of depression.

Research has shown that the amygdala plays a role in clinical depression. The amygdala serves a role in emotional responses to stimuli. The amygdala assigns significance to stimuli determining that stimuli have a strong emotional impact. The orbital cortex acts as a balance to the activity of the amygdala. As the amygdala is an activating agent for emotional response, the orbital cortex is an inhibiting agent to those emotional responses. Studies have shown that individuals suffering from depression have increased activity in the amygdala and reduced activity in the orbital cortex. These two areas provide the hypothalamus with the necessary information as to adjust the activity of the pituitary in secreting ACTH. Since several neurological components play into the regulation of cortisol into the system, breakdowns in several of the areas could result in depression.

Bipolar Disorder patients have been shown a degree of variation when examined for neurological similarities that could produce the disorder. Some research has shown that individuals that have had manic episodes that are symptomatic of bipolar disorder have shown a decrease in grey matter in the temporal lobes and cerebellum after the manic episodes. With such findings, one could conclude that there are significant differences between Depression and Bipolar Disorder. According to the *DSM-IV-TR* (American Psychiatric Association, 2004), unipolar depression and bipolar disorders are grouped together due to the behavioral similarities. Upon examining the neurological bases for the disorders, one can note that bipolar disorder is degenerative in its course while depression is associated with a hormonal imbalance and defective feedback loop with the HPA-axis. A model of bipolar disorder has been hypothesized based on these findings that as the condition progresses the individual would become more sensitive to the effects of the excessive levels of cortisol that result from the depressive episodes with bipolar disorder.

The diagnosis of Bipolar I consists of the individual have at least one manic episode. A Major Depressive Episode is not required, and the absence of a Major Depressive Episode would be noted as being Bipolar I, Single Manic Episode. Major Depressive Episodes usually do occur with Bipolar I but are not required for the diagnosis.

The diagnosis of Bipolar II does require at least one or more Major Depressive Episodes and no Manic Episodes. Bipolar II does require that the individual have experienced at least one Hypomanic Episode .If a Manic Episode occurs, the individual would be considered Bipolar I instead of Bipolar II. Therefore, the difference is that Bipolar I requires a Manic Episode while Bipolar II excludes a Manic Episode and requires a Hypomanic Episode, and Bipolar II requires a Major Depressive Episode while Bipolar I does not.

Neurological Basis of Motor Disorders

Motor Disorders can be divided into two prominent categories of disorders, which consists of hyperkinetic and hypokinetic disorders. Hyperkinetic disorders include Huntington's chorea and Tourette's syndrome. These disorders involve an excessive of motor activity resulting involuntary movements that are in excess of the normal desired movements of the individual. Hypokinetic disorders involve a loss of movement, and the individual often appears to be rigid with regards to movements. This most common hypokinetic disorder is Parkinson's disease.

Huntington's chorea was one of the earliest motor disorders to be described. Huntington's chorea appears to be genetically transmitted from one generation to the next. Upon examining the brain of an individual with Huntington's chorea, the most notable difference between the brain of an individual with the disorder and that of a normal individual is atrophy of the basal ganglia. As the basal ganglia is responsible for the coordination of motor movements, one can denote that the abnormalities in both the size and neuronal structures of the basal ganglia serve as the biological basis for the condition. GABA projections from the basal ganglia to the substantia nigra, glutamate projections from the cortex to the basal ganglia, dopamine projections from the substania nigra to the basal ganglia, and Ach neurons in the basal ganglia appear as the malformed connections in the brains of Huntington's chorea. As the connections also play roles in memory and cognitive functioning, it is common for individuals suffering from the disorder to also show deficits in these areas of functioning in addition to the hyperkinetic motor functioning.

Tourette's syndrome is a disorder that is typically notice early in childhood. The notable symptom of Tourette's syndrome is the presences of tics, which consist of both motor twitch and audible noises. Like Huntington's chorea, Tourette's syndrome has been linked to abnormalities in the basal ganglia. Since antidopaminergic medicines have been effectively used in the treatment of Tourette's syndrome's symptoms, one can that the disorder may have links to abnormalities in the regulation of the neurotransmitter dopamine. Studies of Tourette's syndrome patients postmortem have been inconclusive as the causes of the disorder through autopsy. Some have found abnormalities in the number of neurons in the basal ganglia while other studies have reported no difference.

As Parkinson's disease has received much attention in the media as of recent years, research into the disorder has also received quite a bit of attention. The disorder present symptoms that include tremors, muscular rigidity, and involuntary movements as positive symptoms and difficulty maintaining balance, awkward posturing, impairments of movement, and an absence of voice tone as negative symptoms. The disorder begins to be noticed first in extremities and gradually progresses to more dramatic manifestations of the symptoms in an intermittent fashion with periods of disturbances occurring during certain times and periods lacking symptoms separating times in which the symptoms are progressively increasing. From the onset of the condition, the disorder will progress until the individual is incapacitated by the condition. The progression usually takes ten to twenty years to progress to the point of incapacitation. Parkinson's disease has been linked to several possible causes that include origins as the result of damage from encephalitis, syphilis, carbon monoxide poisoning, manganese intoxication, and drug use. Research suggests a link to damage to the dopaminergic pathways from the substania nigra to the frontal cortex and basal ganglia. Additionally, decreases in norepinephrine and basal ganglia damage have been linked to Parkinson's disease.

Psychosurgery and Medications

As mentioned earlier, the advances in understanding the brain functions has produced drastic changes in the fields of psychology and psychiatry; however, some advances and proposed treatments have been highly controversial. Psychosurgery has been one of the most controversial of these treatments. This procedure involves destroying a section of the brain to improve the condition of an individual. At first, such a concept seems counterproductive as neurons do not grow back and each part of the brain serves multiple functions as has been noted through numerous study and vast research. The idea has been popular at varying times in history. Antonio Moniz was even awarded a Nobel Prize in Medicine in 1949 for his discovery of the lobotomy, which involved cutting the connection to and from the prefrontal cortex (Jansson, 1998). It is important to note that neurosurgery is much different than psychosurgery. In neurosurgery, the goal is to repair damage to decrease symptoms as opposed to damaging brain tissue to relieve symptoms. Concern over the effects of lobotomies and other questionable practices gave rise to the anti-psychiatric movement in 1950s and 1960s. Some of the treatments that spurred that movement survived the movement and continued to be used in limited fashion, but lobotomies are rarely performed today. The procedure is actually illegal to perform in some countries (Shorter, 1998).

In addition to the Anti-Psychiatric Movement, the creation of effective psycho-pharmaceuticals led to the end of psychosurgeries. As a result of the advances in understanding how depression, bipolar disorder, and Schizophrenia affected the mind, medications have been developed to improve the symptoms of such patients in a more effective manner (Stolerman, 2010). In the case of depression, Fluoxetine (Prozac) has been developed for treating depression based on the neurotropic factors of depression. Fluoxetine is a selective serotonin reuptake inhibitor (SSRI). SSRIs produce several changes in the chemistry of the brain. The SSRIs increase the amount of serotonin in the cortex, stimulate BDNF production and neurogenesis in the hippocampus, and provide an increase in granule cells. These changes effect the HPA-axis to bring about a balance to the system and decrease the effects of the elevated levels of cortisol that resulted by the abnormalities that led to the depression. Bipolar patients, however, are highly sensitive to changes in mood-related hormones and neurotransmitters in their system. With patients suffering from Bipolar Disorder, medications such as Lithium and other mood stabilizing drugs have been developed that are most successful in treating Bipolar Disorder.

Schizophrenic Symptoms

Schizophrenia share several common features. Schizophrenia, in general, requires that both positive and negative symptoms are present for a significant portion of time during a one-month period (or less if successfully treated). Some symptoms must occur during a full six-month period. The symptoms will need to cause significant impairment in one or more major functional areas such as work, interpersonal relations, or self-care. These impairments will cause functioning those areas to be markedly below the level that was prior to the onset. The signs of Schizophrenia will be continuous during the 6-month period with at least one month of active symptoms. If a Major Depressive Episode, Manic Episode, or Mixed Episode were to occur during the 6 month period, Schizophrenia would be excluded from being an appropriate diagnosis as a Mood Disorder or Schizoaffective Disorder would be more appropriate. The symptoms also may not be the result of substance abuse or a general medical condition. In the cases of a comorbid pervasive developmental disorder, prominent delusions or hallucinations are required to warrant the diagnosis of any type of Schizophrenia as a comorbid condition.

In considering the different subtypes of Schizophrenia, Schizophrenia, Catatonic Type, is significant from the other types in that it requires certain criteria to be present, and the diagnosis has an absence of exclusion criteria unlike the other sub-types. The requirement for Schizophrenia, Catatonic Type, is that the individual demonstrates at least two of five specific symptoms that include (1) waxy flexibility or a stupor, (2) excessive motor activity that is purposeless and not the result of external stimuli, (3) extreme negativism or mutism, (4) peculiarities of voluntary movements as evidenced by posturing, stereotyped movements, prominent mannerisms, or grimacing, and (5) echolalia or echopraxia. With the other types of Schizophrenia, one will notice that exclusion criteria exists that preclude the presence of the criteria from certain other forms of Schizophrenia that could be seen as the more severe forms. Schizophrenia, Disorganized Type, has the exclusion criteria that requirements of Schizophrenia, Catatonic Type, cannot be met for the particular diagnosis. Schizophrenia, Disorganized Type, does have requirement that disorganized speech, disorganized behavior, and a flat or inappropriate affect must all be prominent features of the individual to warrant the diagnosis. The difference between the catatonic type and the disorganized type is that catatonic type can occur if the criteria are met for both catatonic and disorganized types, but for disorganized type to be given as a diagnosis, the criteria of the catatonic type cannot be met.

Biological Basis of Schizophrenia

The symptoms of Schizophrenia are often divided into positive and negative symptoms. The positive symptoms are characterized by symptoms that produce an excess or distortion to the normal functioning of an individual. These positive symptoms include distortions in the individuals thought content, perception, language, thought processing, and self-monitoring of behavior. The positive symptoms can also be defined as being psychotic or disorganized in nature. The positive symptoms are listed in criteria A1-A4 of the diagnostic criteria for schizophrenia in the DSM-IV-TR.

The negative symptoms of schizophrenia consist of a diminishment or absence of the characteristics an individual associates with normal functioning. These negative characteristics include a flat affect, alogia, or avolition. One will notice that individuals exhibiting negative symptoms appear to be socially withdrawn, lack emotional expressions, lose interest in activities, neglect their hygiene, and lose motivation to carry out activities. The negative symptoms of schizophrenia are listed in criteria A5 of the diagnostic criteria for schizophrenia in the DSM-IV-TR. The fundamental difference between the two types of symptoms is that positive symptoms provide an excess to or distort normal function while negative symptoms detract from the characteristics of normal functioning.

Throughout history, Schizophrenia has served to be one of the most perplexing and bizarre disorders for psychologists, psychiatrists, physicians, and the general public. Historically, attention given to the disorder and the past treatments thereof has served as the force that has created numerous sweeping changes in mental health care. Schizophrenia served as a mystery for decades as patients were warehoused away in asylums like the Bethlem Royal Hospital, the Waverly Hills Sanatorium, the Trans-Allegany Lunatic Asylum, and the Amityville Mental Asylum. Shelving individuals away in dark rooms was the answer to the disorder until research began shedding a light on the cause of the disorder allowing hope for treatment. As the disorder was better understood, changes occurred in the systems that treated the disorder to move from the older forms of simply locking patients away without hope of getting better (Pridemore, 2004).

To understand Schizophrenia at a biological level, one should understand the differences between the brain of an individual suffering from Schizophrenia and a normal, non-schizophrenic individual. The first noticeable difference is that the brain of a schizophrenic patient is lighter on average than the brain of a normal individual. The lighter weight of the brain is the result of smaller frontal lobes due to a lower number of neurons in the prefrontal cortex. Abnormalities were also found in the organization of pyramidal neuronal organization in the hippocampus and fewer synapses between the dorsolateral prefrontal cells. As the frontal lobes play a significant role in higher level thought and organization of thought, one can note that the disorganized and simplistic connections of neurons in the prefrontal regions could have a connection to the delusions that are symptomatic of schizophrenic patients. The haphazard organization of the hippocampal neurons can be seen as possibly contributing to this by providing a misdirected firing of neuronal circuits due to the disorganized layout of the pyramidal cells of this region that plays a key role in memory. With the area of the brain responsible for memory being disorganized, the misfiring of neurons could clearly be seen as resulting from this disorganization. One may argue that plasticity would serve to correct the neuronal misfiring of individuals suffering from Schizophrenia, but in the case of Schizophrenia, neurological functioning may not have been affected in such a way that biological processes would necessarily restructure the neural pathways in a corrective manner as could be seen in some cases of head trauma, split-brain patients, and various other incidents that involve neural plasticity.

The reduced prefrontal cortex mass in schizophrenics also interferes with the body's regulation of dopamine, which serves an important role in reward and pleasure. A pathway exists between the prefrontal cortex and the tegmental area. This pathway functions to trigger the release of dopamine into the body. As this pathway is affected by the reduced connections in the prefrontal cortex, the individual is deprived of the neurotransmitter that reinforces positive experience

which would serve to produce goal oriented drive toward things of interest and positive emotions. As this pathway is disrupted, several of the negative symptoms of Schizophrenia would occur such as loss of interest or drive, normal responses, and blunted emotions or a flat affect.

Factious, Malingering, and

Somatoform

Factitious Disorder is separated from malingering by the motives for the feigning of illness. An individual that is malingering illness is motivated to feign illness by a secondary gain. This secondary gain is often monetary but can also include avoiding required duties or punishment. A person may malinger to avoid military service, civil duties, jail time, or other similar requirements. A person may malinger to gain disability benefits, worker compensation, or a reward in a lawsuit.

Individuals with Factitious Disorder feign illness not for secondary gain such as monetary compensation or avoiding of obligations. A person with Factitious Disorder fakes illness to assume the role of a sick person. Their motives are the attention that comes from being a patient or being ill. In the case of Factitious

Disorder, the individual can also impose the role of the patient on a person that is close to them. This often occurs with women who have their children fake an illness to garner sympathy from others.

With malingering and Factitious Disorder, the individual does not have any physical symptoms that suggest a medical condition. On the other hand, Somatoform Disorders have the presence of physical symptoms that suggest a general medical condition, but the reported symptoms are not fully explained by a true medical condition, the direct effect of a substance, or another mental disorder. Somatoform Disorders typically involve the exacerbation of symptoms or the amplification of reported problems that are produced by a general medical condition. The major difference between Somatoform Disorders and Factitious Disorder or malingering is the actual presence of a medical condition.

Personality Disorders

Obsessive Compulsive Personality Disorder is characterized by a preoccupation with orderliness and neatness. This type of personality disorder is noted as being characterized by a pervasive and enduring pattern of inflexibility in adhering to rules and perfectionistic tendencies. This diagnosis requires the presence of four or more symptoms. These symptoms include rigidity and stubbornness; a miserly spending style toward self and others, reluctance in delegating tasks; inability to discard worthless objects even when they have no sentimental value; inflexible about morality, ethics, and values; excessively devoted to work and excludes leisurely activities; perfectionism that interferes with task completion; and preoccupation with rules, details, lists, order, and organization to the degree where the point of the task is lost. The typical onset for this disorder is in adolescence or early adulthood and causes distress and impairment in daily activities.

The prime example of OCPD is the character Rabbit from the Winnie the Pooh stories. Rabbit is overly preoccupied with arranging the carrots in his garden in an orderly manner to the point that he never finishes arranging them. He always speaks of working and not having time for leisurely activities. Whenever there is a task that needs done, Rabbit will spend so much time organizing and planning that the task does not get started. He directs others around in a miserly manner. Rabbit personifies the traits of OCPD in each facet to the point that he clearly be defined as OCPD.

A high level of emotional reactivity and attention-seeking behaviors characterizes Histrionic Personality Disorder. This disorder is indicated by the presence of five or more symptoms that include discomfort in situations where they are not the center of attention, inappropriate sexually seductive or provocative behavior, rapidly shifting and shallow expressions and emotions, uses physical appearance to gain attention, excessively impressionistic and shallow style of speech, self-dramatization, highly suggestible, and considers relationships to be more intimate than they are. Histrionic Personality Disorder typically begins in early adulthood and presents an enduring long-term pattern with inflexibility in the behaviors and thought patterns of the individual that cause distress and impairment. The severity of the symptoms denotes that the pattern of behavior and though clearly deviates from the expectations of the culture.

A prime example of Histrionic Personality Disorder is Jessica Rabbit from *Who Framed Roger Rabbit?* (Zemeckis, 1988). Jessica Rabbit clearly dresses provocatively and craves attention. One can note that she changes the subject of conversation so that the focus of a conversation will return back to her be the topic. Her relationship with Roger Rabbit is described by her using great amount of detail that is completely abstract. In addition, the depth of their relationship truly involved him just making her laugh as opposed to the dramatic but shallow depiction she provided of their relationship. Her appearance is also used repeatedly to draw attention back to herself.

Cognitive Disorders

With examining the differences between the three disorders, one should first consider what the symptoms of delirium are. Delirium can be seen as a brief but global cognitive impairment. As compared to dementias, which are chronic disorders, delirium is a short-term disorder. Delirium develops over the course of hours to days and typically completes its course within weeks. This type of course can be seen as transient in delirium.

Unlike both dementia and amnestic disorders, delirium does not require memory impairments even though memory impairments can be seen in delirium. With dementias, impairment in memory is required for diagnosis along with one other cognitive deficit. As compared to amnestic disorders, dementias and deliriums require impairments of cognitive functioning while such impairments in cognitive functioning is required to be excluded from the diagnosis of amnestic disorders. With amnestic disorders, the course can be specified as *Chronic* or *Transient* unlike dementias and deliriums that are restricted to only one course of chronic in the case of dementia and transient in the case of delirium.

In considering the similarities between the disorders, one can note that each disorder produces some type of impairment for the individual. Amnestic disorders and dementias share the requirement of memory impairment while dementias and delirium share the requirement of cognitive impairment. Additionally, one can note that each group of disorders is then divided into their individual disorders based on the indicated etiology that results in the associated impairments that are indicative of the disorder category.

The two most common types of dementia are Dementia of the Alzheimer's Type and Vascular Dementia. Both types present impairment in memory coupled with at least one other cognitive deficit. The other cognitive impairment can include Aphasia (a cognitive impairment in language), Apraxia (an impairment in motor skills), Agnosia (an impairment in recognizing or naming objects), or impairment in executive functioning (an impairment in planning or abstract higher level thought). In both disorders, the impairment caused by the cognitive deficits cause significant impairment in social or occupational functioning and represent a serious decline from the previous level of functioning. Additionally, these deficits do not occur exclusively during the course of delirium.

In the case of Dementia of the Alzheimer's Type, the course is characterized by a gradual onset that has a continuing cognitive decline. Vascular Dementia, on the other hand, develops in a stepwise manner. In fully explaining the difference in the progression of cognitive decline, one can refer to the below chart that demonstrates the difference between a stepwise regression as is seen in Vascular Dementia and the gradual decline that is seen in Dementia of the Alzheimer's Type. In addition to the onset and course of the dementias, the two dementias differ in their etiologies. In the case of Vascular Dementia, signs are present that would indicate the symptoms appear to be the result of cerebrovascular disease. The etiology can be demonstrated through the presence of focal neurological signs and symptoms such as exaggerated deep tendon reflexes, extensor plantar response, pseudo bulbar palsy, gait abnormalities, and the weakness of an extremity. Dementia of the Alzheimer's Type serves to be a diagnosis of exclusion in that this diagnosis is given when all other factors (Cerebrovascular disease, central nervous system conditions that result in such symptoms, and substance induced conditions) have been determined not to be etiologically responsible for the disturbances.

Dementia is a concern for many people as a large portion of the population is approaching old age. A person who has dementia must show impairments in memory. Usually this begins with having trouble remembering new information and then progresses to loss of older memories. Additionally, individuals suffering from dementia will have at least one other cognitive deficit such as aphasia, apraxia, agnosia, or a disturbance of executive functioning.

Aphasia is a difficulty in communicating. There are two common types of aphasias. Broca's Aphasia is referred to as an expressive aphasia because the person will understand you, but they will have difficulty communicating to you. This is not due to a speech impediment. They simply have trouble communicating what they want to say. The second type of aphasia is Wernicke's Aphasia. This is considered a receptive type of aphasia. In this case, the individual is unable to understand what is being conveyed to them even though their hearing is fine. Typically, what they hear sounds like a "word salad" that does not make sense. They will still be able to communicate to you though.

The second cognitive deficit is apraxia. Apraxia is an impairment of motor functions or movements. This can be seen as an impairment of gross motor movement which can be seen large movements such as walking and running. Additionally, fine motor movements can be impaired which include things such as writing and precise small movements. Often fine motor apraxia that affects the vocal cords can be confused with aphasia, but it is more correctly identified as apraxia.

The third type of cognitive deficit is agnosia. Agnosia is an inability to identify things such as people, objects, and other items that a person would normally have an easy time identifying. Prosopagnosia is the inability to remember faces and names of people. A humorous example is that of the man who mistook his wife for a hat and actually attempted put his wife on his head.

The impairments of executive functioning can be seen as impairments in the person's ability to plan things. These individuals may have difficulty put clothing on in the correct order or planning the day's activities in a logical manner. For instance, the person may have confuse the correct steps needed to return.

Therapy

It seems that psychoanalysis seems to be held back by its lack of cost-effectiveness. This seems to be a major issue due to the fact that an insurer or an individual would not want to pay out $60,000 for treatment when there could be less expensive alternatives. The issue with cost seems to be one of the factors spurred so much interest in other means of therapy. In addition to the cost factor for treatment, the effectiveness of psychoanalysis seems to have been brought into question numerous times throughout the years. Since psychoanalysis is based on introspection, it seems that it would be almost impossible to replicate studies from one person to another simply due to the uniqueness of each individual. In considering the uniqueness of individuals, psychoanalysis seems to bring attention to that uniqueness that seems to be lacking from some later approaches. Humans seem to be unique in their thoughts and behaviors from one person to the next. There does not seem to be one formula that can answer the same problem of one person to the next. Investing a great deal of time into an individual may be necessary in some circumstances. It seems that listening to the problems of the individual and assisting the individual in finding a way to resolve those issues or cope with those issues may be highly productive. The approach does not seem appropriate in all solutions as can be noted by the author. It does seem that bringing an individual into a realization of their issues may be moving in the right direction. What seems to lack in psychoanalysis is the guidance and directions that some people need when those issues are discovered. This shortcoming seems to be a major issue for the psychoanalytical approach. It brings the issues of an individual to light so that they can cope with the issue, but it does not seem to have a next step. The answer for what to do if the individual does not know how to handle this realization is a key puzzle piece missing from the psychoanalytical approach.

When considering psychoanalysis for an approach, it is usually best to dissect the approach into several pieces. Once the psychoanalysis is dissected into its various components, one can utilize the parts of it as one sees fit. Some parts can be taken in their literal sense; some parts can be taken metaphorically; and some parts can be left on the table and not utilized. One can easily note several parts of the approach to include catharsis, defense mechanisms, Tabula rasa, connections to childhood, Oedipal complex, and psychosexual stages to name a few of the parts that the approach divided into. As has been noted by several others, Freud did have some unusual connections that he made to few childhood experiences and fantasies which may not be for some. These odd connections may have created a stigma which has been attached to the profession, but several of the methods utilized by psychoanalysis can still be quite useful in certain scenarios.

Some of the contributions that have been made by psychoanalysts have left a profound impact upon the profession. The psychosexual stages of development, accurate or inaccurate, lay the groundwork for appreciating the way in which individuals develop through several sequential stages in life. This approach has had a clear influence on many latter therapeutic approaches. In addition to the stages of development, psychoanalysis also addresses the latency of prior events in life and how they impact an individual's current perception and thought processes. When breaking apart the approach into its functional components, the practice of psychotherapy can easily be brought into the current century, at least partly.

In consideration of psychoanalysis, one must also consider the sociological changes that have occurred since Freud's age. The Victorian Era had vastly different values, morals, and ethics than today. Once some of the underlying definitions and societal expectations upon which psychoanalysis was built is modified to fit with current times, the approach and mindset of the therapy can be used in a more effective manner in modern times. Such changes would impact the way in which the id, ego, and superego are viewed. The conflicts between individual desires and societal pressures are still present in current times. The difference is concerning what composes those individual desires and societal pressures. In addressing such slight updates to psychoanalysis, the approach could become more user-friendly in the current era.

The Psychodynamic Approach.

With consideration of Adlerian therapy, one of the most prolific contributions would be Adler's shift from a focus on prior events determining the individual's psychological state to focus on the drive of the individual toward a goal. Freud focused on the past affecting the present while Adler looked at the direction in which an individual is heading. As one comes to realize fictional finalism, the client can then begin to cope with whether that finalism is rational or irrational. The connection between goals and psychological states seems to be much closer of a connection than prior experience and the psychological state of an individual. People act based on purpose, direction, and motivation. Fictional finalisms directly impact all three of these components.

Meanwhile, Freud's focus on prior experiences addresses mainly the elements that had an impact on an individual's drive and reasoning behind reaching a certain goal. It could be possible that an individual would still maintain the same fictional finalism even after coming to terms with the prior experiences that led the individual to desire such a fictional finalism. An extreme example of a finalism effecting behavior would be an individual abusing pain pills in order to achieve a high. The individual's behavior is more influenced by the desire of achieving the end goal of "getting high" as opposed to past experiences with medications. The attention that Adler gave to a goal-driven perspective allows for easier connection to be made between the actions individuals do and the forces that drive those behaviors or thoughts.

In Adler's approach, he does not neglect the causes that lead to an individual developing such fictional finalism. There is an assumption that individuals strive for levels of superiority. The avoidance of inferiority is what causes an individual to develop finalism as goals that create behaviors and thought processes. In laying out this model of how prior experiences lead to goals that lead to behavior, Adler provides the therapist with an understanding of the process of reasoning that leads to abnormality and discomfort. In understanding this pathway, a therapist is able to identify which parts of the pathway serve to be problematic for the client. Upon identifying the issue, steps can be taken to modify the connections that the client has made through reasoning and re-education which can lead to a change in the client's style of life or understanding.

Expectations in Behavioral Therapy

Behaviorist therapies seem to place the least emphasis on the therapeutic relationship, however this neglect does not allow for there to be no relationship at all. The relationship is different and may often vary in application according to the behavioral techniques that are being utilized. Behavioral therapies use a different vocabulary than many other therapies concerning the relationship. Modeling is often used by behavioral therapist in which a relationship would be useful in producing better effects. Processes such as extinction assume that there is a relationship in which the client desires attention or rewards from an individual in response for certain actions. When the actions do not invoke such a response, the behavior is extinguished. Without an initial relationship of understanding on the part of the therapist and desires on the part of the client. This process would not be fully achieved. Therefore, a relationship can also be seen as important for behaviorist even though it may be indirectly emphasized in many situations.

Expectations would play a key role in situations in which an individual seeks out therapy. Assertiveness training and social skills training would be good examples of the types of situations in which expectations would affect the outcome of behavioral therapy. If an individual realizes these types of improvements are needed and seeks therapy to aid them, the individual would be more receptive to such training. Behavioral therapists and researchers have conducted numerous studies to attempt to overcome these concerns with expectations, however, many questions have been thus raised about the expectations and biases of the researchers. This brings the discussion back to the idea that if an individual believes that a treatment will does it mean that treatment will be more likely to work? This seems like something that could have a strong impact on the effectiveness of a treatment but can also serve as a device by which to measure how effective a treatment is.

A quick explanation of things to consider when using reinforcers to modify behaviors.

When considering the reinforcers, one must take into account how effective the reinforcers are to the individual. If a reinforcers are used, they should be relevant to the individual and be coupled appropriately with the behavior that is desired to be reinforced. It seems that often there is an issue with what the reinforcers are associated with for the client. A therapist may intend for the reinforcers to be coupled with an appropriate behavior, but the client may make a connection between the reinforcer and an unintended behavior. In addition, one must consider that often attention is a reinforcer in itself. A person may think that they are attempting to negatively reinforce a behavior, but unintentionally amplify the behavior. Often this can be used to explain how that punishment is not very effective. Also one should consider to make sure that punishment is separated from the reinforcer. If bad behaviors take away from good behaviors, this could discourage the individual from performing good behaviors due to an overwhelming amount of bad behaviors that the individual would have to make up for. In coupling reinforcers and punishment in this manner, the reinforcer is disempowered.

Discovering Albert Ellis in the best possible way.

Emotions drive the manner in which people think about things. Individuals tend to tie emotions to memories. Memories are influence the manner in which people develop beliefs. This beliefs are highly effected by the emotions connected to the memories. To modify the irrational beliefs an individual develops, one would have to break the connections between the memories, emotions, and beliefs created by those memories and emotions. A person may have visited the circus when they were young. While at the circus, they may have experienced a traumatic event or received distressing news. The event or news would have produced fear or sadness. This sadness and fear may have then been associated with trips to circuses. The connection would seem irrational, but a connection that can easily be understood when considering the circumstance and connection between the events and emotions. To change an individual's beliefs, one could direct the individual to consider the connections in a rational manner as opposed to irrationally making the connection between the emotion and the trip to the circus. This shows how cognition and emotions are tied together. Often the experiences and connection will not be readily recognizable to the individual concerning such irrational connections.

To look at emotions, beliefs, and cognitions, one must consider the relationship among the three elements. None of these items happen in a vacuum. The ABC's of cognitive therapy are the activating events, beliefs, and consequences. Emotions are driven by beliefs, and beliefs are created by activating events. A behaviorist would look at the relationship as Stimulus = Response. Strangely enough psychoanalysis usually examines the concept in a similar manner. The events that occur between the stimulus and response are called intervening variables. Typically, they are explained using numerous cognitive models that explain specific events that lead to the end result. Behaviorists claim that these intervening events cannot be measured or understood. Therefore, behaviorists disregard these events that occur in the mind of the individual. These occurrences are what make up cognitions, beliefs, and emotions. If these events are disregarded, humans become mechanistic in nature. If humans were mechanistic, psychology would be nothing more than a simple equation. Changing individuals would boil down to simply a chemical reaction that would always be predictable. Over hundreds of years, we have come to understand that humans are not as easily explainable or predictable as a chemical reaction. Therefore, these intervening mechanisms explain that there are individual differences that should be respected as we cannot fully measure them but are fully aware of their presence and the effect that they have upon human behavior. Within the cognitions and the connections that each person makes or fails to make, emotions are developed. These emotions are influenced and directed by the beliefs that individuals hold. As the beliefs are changed, the direction and likelihood of resulting emotions are redirected, inhibited, and amplified by varying degrees that depend upon the context of the change to beliefs. To disrupt irrational connections between events and emotions, one can change those beliefs, and with effort, the change can carry over to be generalized to other modes of thought that are irrational.

Strong Points of the Gestalt Approach

Some of the techniques that are used by Gestaltist therapist are very useful throughout several different approaches to therapy. The empty chair technique seems like bars some resemblances to the tabula rasa of psychoanalysis. With the empty chair technique, the individual seems to have an easier slate upon which to write because the slate is a chair that is inanimate allowing the client to imagine the person associated with the issue more flexibly. The exercise of "I take responsibility" seems to have connections to existential therapy and could be a useful manner for one to address that existential void. Many of the other techniques seem to allow the client to realize the peculiar mindset in which they are operating. With the exercises of the Gestalt therapists, the useful piece of the exercises are that they get the client into the present. If psychologist had time machines, the past could be fixed very easily with changes of prior experiences. They do not currently have access to such device unfortunately.

Gestalt therapy brings the client into the present which is more feasible than time travel. As the client works through unresolved issues of the past, the therapy pulls him into the present, which is where people live every day. As the client steps away from a mindset of the past and into the present, some of the issues from the past are brought with them. The issues that are brought with them can be cleared up by some of the Gestaltist exercises.

Understanding the void is painful.

The existential void is that which is of greatest concern in the existential approach. I feel that the text does not devote nearly enough time to explaining the concept of the void. Once the void is understood, the rest of the concept will fall into place. The void is simply non-existence. To not exist is very difficult to understand. It can be very upset if one attempts to fully grasp this concept of non-existence. In religious terms, the void can be compared to hell or the Jewish concept of Sheol, which translates to the grave. The concept of sensory deprivation (a state in which all stimuli are removed) can be also used as a good understanding of the existential void. Many times, death is used as a metaphor for understanding the void.

As an example, I will use a dark lake for the void. The void is much like a lake because an individual cannot see what is under the water. Staying above the water in this lake is not an option. One only has the option to go under the dark water and into the unknown mystery that lies underneath the surface. One cannot say that which is in the darkness is neither good nor bad because one does not know what is in the darkness of the deep. One looks out across the lake in the darkness of the deep water and that uncertainty is scary. The unknown is frightening. What is in the unknown could be pleasant or terrible, but simply not knowing makes the unknown extremely terrifying. This fear produces anxiety in some, depression in some, and various other reactions in others. The void must be crossed. It is unavoidable.

To give meaning to the void is to conquer the void. In logotherapy, this is achieved by assigning some purpose to the trials that one goes through to make it through that void of uncertainty. In ascribing meaning to the trials, the turmoil associated with such trials is reduced. Upon making through the void, one emerges on the other side of the lake. On the other side, the individual is a different person. It is possible that they are better, and it is possible that they are worse than before the void. They are simply different and changed by the experience of surviving the void and coming out on the other side in a state of still existing. Once this is understood, the other concepts of existential therapy will make much more sense.

SURVIVING MAKES US BETTER.

Friedrich Nietzsche, the existential philosopher, said, "That which does not kill us makes us stronger." The saying is true to an extent. In relation to making it through the void, one is not always stronger on the other side. One is simply changed. There is a latent danger concerning the "other side of the void." This relates to fictional finalisms in a way. Frankle (2006) explained the condition of men that had survived Nazi concentration camps after they were released. This men spent years thinking that once they were released their suffering would be over. They only found that upon liberation they faced a whole new set of challenges in integrating back into a regular society. This can be seen as relevant when considering PTSD whether it be a veteran returning from war, a rape victim, or even a prisoner upon release. During the experienced trauma, the meaning that drives the individual to continue surviving is the hope that there is relief at the end of the experience. When the end is reach and new challenges are faced, the individual has a new void that they find themselves having to confront. We find that life is a void in itself. If there is no meaning to the daily suffering experienced in life, hope would be lost, and the individual would surrender. When working with elderly clients, this understanding of the void would also be of great use. Erikson (1950) proposed that in later life the conflict occurs where an individual must come to terms with the contributions they made during their lifetimes. The conflict will produce either a state of despair or wisdom. Elderly clients have crossed many voids during their life. Typically, they will look back at the past experiences and use the results of prior crossings to judge their crossing of the ultimate void of death. To combat the despair of the elderly and the suffering of the PTSD sufferer, a new meaning can be ascribed to the new trials that are faced. Some degree of suffering will be present throughout life and death. To forget this and then be reminded is distressing for many.

However, the degree to which one suffers in life can be diminished if the individual understands the reason that he suffers and is given a goal for surviving the suffering.

Carl Roger's Approach to Therapy.

The relationship between the client and therapist in Carl Rogers' person-centered therapy seems like a bit of a balancing act, but the strategy seems to have a clear meaning as to why the approach is useful. Rogers lays out six conditions for the relationship which make sense. Most important among these six points seems to be the themes of genuineness, positive regard, and empathy. Genuineness prevents the client from turning against the therapist. If the client believes the therapist to not be sincere, the client will question the therapist's motives and purpose. Therapy sessions would be either become unproductive or counterproductive if the client does not regard the therapist as being straightforward and genuine. In having unconditional positive regard, the therapist is encouraging the client to realize that they do have worth, and this serves as a device by which the client is freed from their conditions of worth that they perceive they must adhere. Empathy (not sympathy) serves to make a connection between the client and therapist. This connection reinforces the effects of the positive regard of therapist to the client. This understanding allows for the client to see that even with their shortcomings in the open the therapist still maintains positive regard. The effect of this reduces the anxieties that have been caused by incongruences between the current state of the client and the client's perceived goal state that is actually seen as a level of worthiness by the client. Through these strategies, person-centered therapy effectively addresses psychological issues in manner that focuses on achieving a better quality of living for the client.

Interpersonal Therapy.

In IPT, the concept of role dispute poses an interesting concept. In examining role disputes, one must consider how these disputes originate, or more appropriately, how the incompatible expectations originate. For example, consider a couple with issues of infidelity. An individual does not enter a relationship with the intention of cheating on his or her partner. The problem that leads to this situation begins when the two first meet. Each individual has a list of what they want or need from a pattern in their mind. This list may be something that he or she is aware of or not. Typically, it is not something that is explicitly created by the person. They will also have a list of what they believe the other person expects from them.

So the two people meet and the relationship begins as relationships typically do. It begins with a few white lies by each person and few things each person does a few things to attempt to compensate for their perceived inferiorities as Adler would say. These white lies may not seem like such a big deal at the time but time has a way of magnifying things to larger sizes. Therefore, no one wants to be caught up in a lie even if it is about their own personality. Other lies are told to the partner and the each individual lies to his or herself also. The relationship is begun on a foundation of lies. Each person is living in a world of lies so that the lists are completely checked off and all needs are satisfied. Unfortunately, the art of keeping up with lies is pretty exhausting. The people eventually get tired and the truth comes out. It is never really addressed, but some of the items on the list get unchecked. This creates deficits for the individuals and also creates a longing for the list items to be satisfied again. Over time, the longing grows stronger. Sometimes, the individuals begin to unintentionally and sometimes intentionally search for those items that they are missing. Other times, the individuals simply become bitter toward one another due to feeling that the other might be to blame for their missing those items off of their list.

An interesting approach that I have seen done before with cases such as these is to have the individuals make out their lists of what is important to them in a partner. Once the lists are made out, each will compare their partner to the list to see which are items are checked off and which are missing. After this is done, each person will go down the list of missing items and ask two simple questions about each missing item. First, they should ask if the lack of that attribute will affect how they function as a couple, and secondly, they will ask if the lack of that attribute affects how they care about each other. I have seen the exercise modified for different types of roles and relationships, but it does serve in raising awareness among individuals about interpersonal issues.

Surviving as a Common Thread.

It seems that the common thread among these techniques would be for the individual to survive the experience in a manner that is de-catastrophizing. I don't think I can put it any better than a professor told me before on the first day of classes in college when he said, "It is amazing how much you can take. You just don't know it." That was on the first day of class. That seems to be a common thread that I missed earlier. Therapy assists individuals in coming to this conclusion that they can take what they are going through. To do this, these techniques expose an individual to that which causes their distress and suffering. In psychoanalysis, one confronts a controlling parent who is played by the psychoanalyst using the blank slate technique. They vent and work through the issue. This puts the problem back in the past and out of the present. In Rogerian terms, the conditions and expectations which Rogers believed to be that which was caused by prior experiences. As the individual survives the showing of his real self to therapist, the therapist uses unconditional positive regard and genuineness to deflate the worry caused by the unmet expectations of the client.

Exposure therapy seems to combine this ideas in a way. The experiences are re-lived or duplicated either in a manner that progresses. As the individual experiences prolonged exposure to that which causes anxiety and distress, nothing happens to him or her physically. They realize that the fears they held were irrational. As the exposure is continued, the fear subsides and loses its power over the individual. The approaches have different explanations of how this process takes place. They use vastly different terminology, but in the end, the result and process is highly similar. Figure out what the problem is. Confront the problem. Survive it. Finally, realize that it was as bad as imagined and realize that the problem is no longer a problem.

Existing Connections among Therapeutic Approaches.

It seems that the common underlying theme of all the therapeutic theories is to manipulate the understanding and thinking of individuals for the purpose of assisting individuals in functioning from day to day. The debate between different theorists seems to be centered on whether or not a specific approach produces positive results. It can clearly be noted that the connections between the various schools of thought seem to be significant when considering first how the therapist forms a relationship with the patient/client to allow for the individual to open up to the suggested change. This dispute among therapists seems to be one of the contributing factors to the creation of so many different schools of thought on psychotherapy. Since each therapy has individuals both attacking and defending it, young therapists entering the field are more apt to feel that they stand a better chance of creating an approach that is unique in some way but still holds similarities to the schools in which they were trained in originally. As this process has been drug out over the course of one hundred years, the number of therapies has grown in a similar pattern to how the field has grown. As new therapies have emerged from individuals who were trained in older schools of psychotherapy, it is clear that certain factors still are relevant in each of the new therapies. These common threads seem to be the things that all parties agree are fundamentally important in psychotherapy.

Expectations and a therapeutic relationship seem to be the two most prolific threads that go throughout all forms of psychotherapy. Any individual that comes to a therapist has some expectations concerning the outcome of the treatment. If there were no expectation or hope for improvement, there would most likely be no attempt for the therapy to be sought out as a treatment in the first place. In the majority of therapies, it seems that positive expectations would result in an improved chance at success. Secondly, the therapeutic relationship serves to be a necessity in any psychotherapy. Without some type of positive relationship, it seems that the client or patient would be more resistant to treatment, and the therapy would be less effective. Due to this fact, a positive relationship consistently appears across different therapies.

Transference in Freudian Therapy

Transference does allow one to vent and release frustrations. In addition this, there is a second aspect of transference which is raising of awareness. Through the process of transference, one becomes more fully aware of the feelings, emotions, and reasoning that they have held back. When they vent and say those things out loud, they are able to realize the connections that have in their unconscious. It is important to remember that the unconscious does not reason things logically. Thoughts in the unconscious are often ridiculous in the connections that are made. Once one realizes the connections that they make and how the problems they are currently experiencing are connected, they can begin to work through their problems and make sense of things. Transference is a step in the process of improving the quality of life.

First one will vent about the issue. This will cause one to realize what they are thinking. Next, think through what you are thinking in a more logical manner than the unconscious methods that one typically uses. This will allow one to address the issue. Through this addressing of the issue, one will create and evaluate alternative solutions to the situations. After creating several alternatives, one will choose whether to change his or her thinking or to continue along the same pattern of thinking. Finally, one will implement such a change in thinking and apply it to day-to-day life.

This is a model of how the venting in transference could create improvements for the individual. It could be modified due to transference being a unique process for each person but this could serve as a general overview.

Summarizing It All

Throughout this book, we have taken a long some of the prominent psychological disorders to allow for a better understanding of how certain disorders such as anxiety, depression, and schizophrenia affect the individual and their patterns of though. This conditions clearly do affect functioning on a daily basis for the people who suffer from them. In addition to examining the conditions, we have examined some of the approaches one can take to treating such disorders.

Some of the approaches that are mentioned in popular culture such as Freudian approaches to therapy are not actually used in most therapist's offices. When one receives treatment for most conditions, a therapist will use more rational approaches such as Cognitive Behavioral Therapy that have been grounded in scientific research than what is commonly presented in television and movies. The arm chairs and couches have been turned in for a more hands on approach to treatment. The act of treating individuals and bettering their quality of life is truly hard work. The information that has been covered in this book provides and overview of some disorders and treatments. It is very important to remember that there is a great deal more to this conditions and treatments than what can simply be put together in a few brief pages. Research will contradict and conflict with other research when regarding the way the mind of an individual due to the complexities of the workings of the human mind that has such an amazing design.

I urge each and every reader to delve more into the studies of the mind for the purposes of both support and challenging existing research, my views, and the views of all people who have came before me so that we will have the opportunity to better understand the incredible way in which people think and behave. If we, as human beings, are fortunate enough then one day we might just grasp enough of an understanding about psychological processes to truly realize how the mind fully works and the psychological problems that are very real for so many people who suffer from them daily.